The Pigeon & T

Friendship, Jealousy, and Courage

In the heart of New York City, atop the tallest tree in Central Park, stood the neigh-bird-hood of Birdhattan.

All the birds of the park lived there, from the most colorful of cardinals to the grayest of pigeons.

They sang together and ate together and were happy together, coming up with new games to play every day.

One bird was determined to be in charge of coming up with the games, as well as deciding when to play them. His name was **Pepper Pigeon**, and he had gray feathers that stood out amidst the leaves.

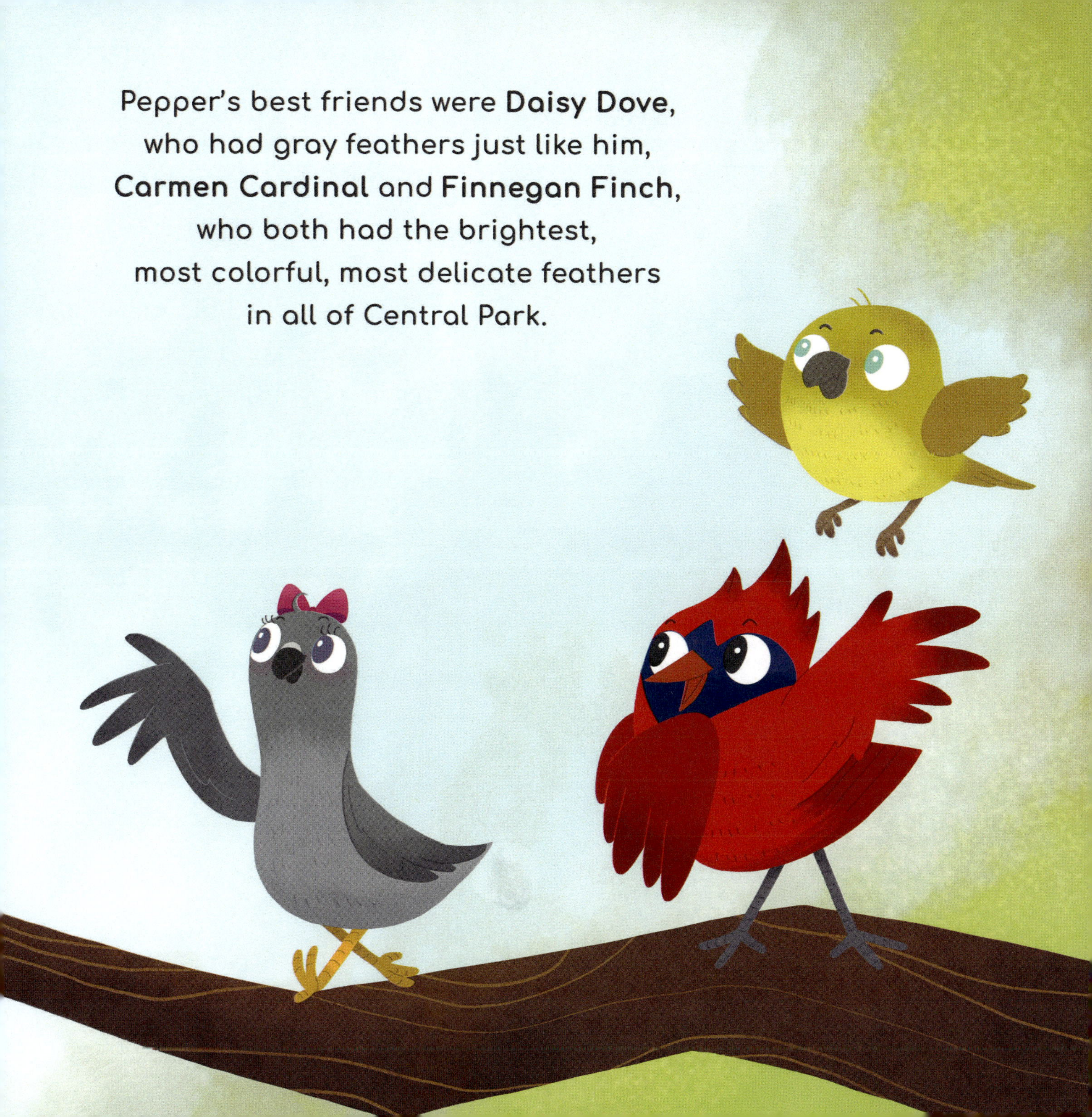

Pepper's best friends were **Daisy Dove**,
who had gray feathers just like him,
Carmen Cardinal and **Finnegan Finch**,
who both had the brightest,
most colorful, most delicate feathers
in all of Central Park.

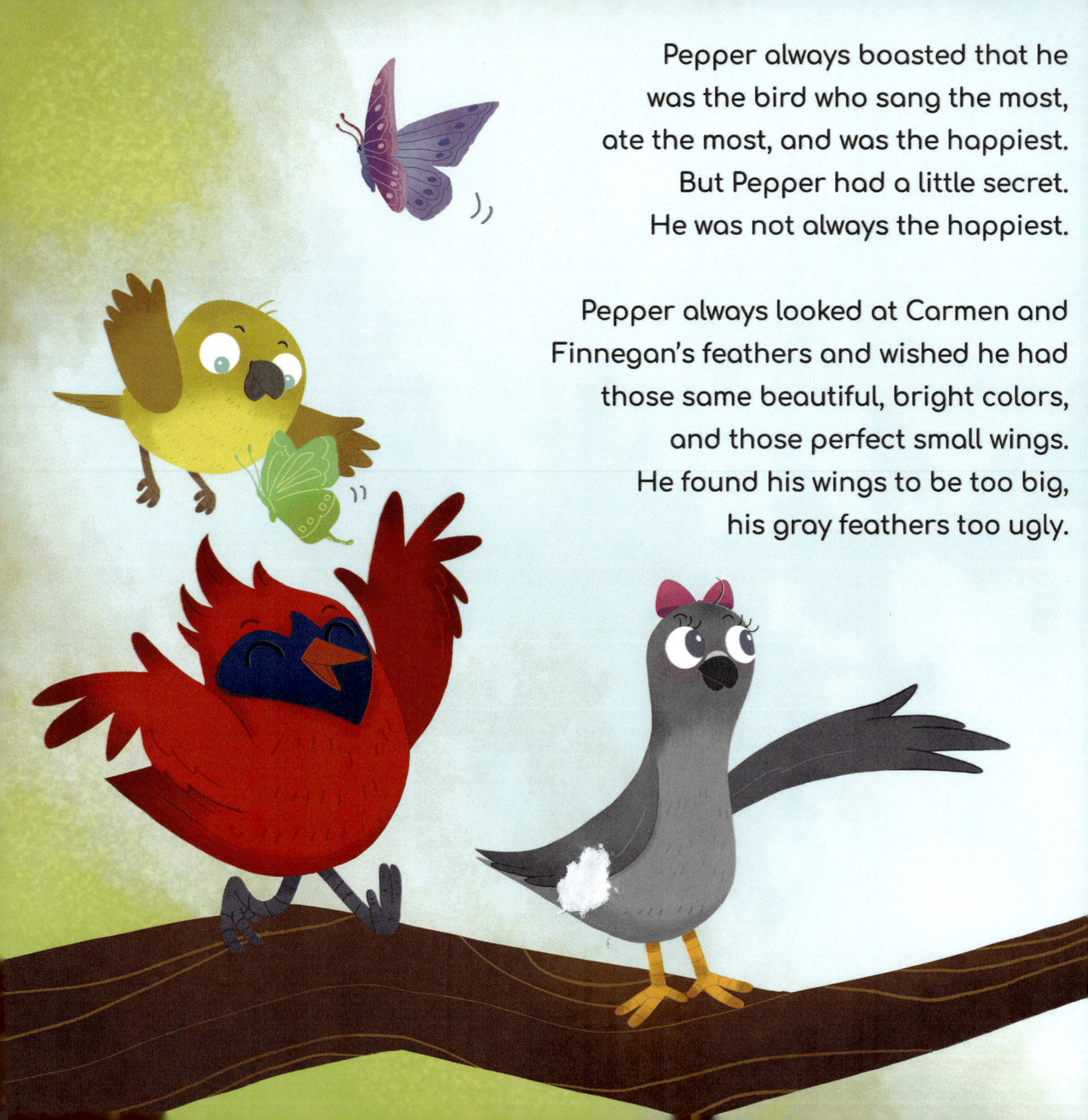

Pepper always boasted that he
was the bird who sang the most,
ate the most, and was the happiest.
But Pepper had a little secret.
He was not always the happiest.

Pepper always looked at Carmen and
Finnegan's feathers and wished he had
those same beautiful, bright colors,
and those perfect small wings.
He found his wings to be too big,
his gray feathers too ugly.

Daisy tried to get her friend to think his gray feathers were just as beautiful as all the other colorful feathers in the park.

"Forget about that, silly," she said.

"Just come and play with us!"

Pepper heard Daisy's words, but he still felt sad whenever he looked at Carmen and Finnegan.

To make his heart happy, Pepper always came up with silly things to stand out among his friends. He would make funny faces to make his friends laugh.

He looked for shiny items around the park and wore them as funky hats, even if they were sticky. He did dangerous tricks to keep his friends' eyes on him, even if he really did not want to do them.

And he AAALWAYS decided what they played, and how they played it. As long as he was in charge and people listened to him, everything was OK. Pepper felt his friends loved him and he was happy.

One day,
while playing at
the **Central Park Zoo,**
Pepper and his friends saw
Mr. McGoose, the zookeeper, bring in a huge box.
Pepper, Daisy, Carmen, and Finnegan stared in awe,
imagining what could be inside. But they did not go
near the box while Mr. McGoose was nearby, for
they were scared of being seen and caught by
the Big Orange Cat. The Big Orange Cat did
not like when birds from the park were in the
zoo, and it was his job to scare them away.

Once Mr. McGoose and the Big Orange Cat had left, Pepper and his friends flew down to inspect the mysterious box.

"What could it be?" asked Pepper.
"It must be a new animal," said Finnegan.
"Maybe a penguin!" exclaimed Carmen.
"Maybe a seal!" declared Daisy.

They could all see just a small hint of blue and green feathers peeking from the shadows of the box. Pepper had never seen feathers as pretty as these. ***"Ex-coo-se me,"*** said Daisy as she flew down and sat on top of the box. ***"Knock, knock, knock. Who are you?"***

From out the shadows came dashing, bright feathers of the strongest blue and the strongest green Pepper had ever seen! A long, bright blue neck followed, that looked down upon Pepper and his friends. ***"My name is Preston Peacock,"*** said the strange creature in a deep voice, ***"and I am new to the zoo."***

He slowly climbed out of his cage, and as he did, the whole gang gasped at his enormous tail. Pepper couldn't even count the amount of colors that were painted into it!

"Welcome to Central Park!" said Daisy with a smile. ***"Would you like to play with us?"***

"Alright," said Preston. ***"But only if we play duck, duck, goose, for that is the only game I like to play."***

"Oh, wow!" said Carmen Cardinal. ***"What an amazing tail!"***

"I know," said Preston with a smile. ***"It came very in handy for my days skydiving in Spain."***

The friendly birds 'oohed' and 'aahed', but Pepper didn't even know what a Spain was. All his friends seemed so happy, and he felt his cheeks getting redder and redder.

Over the next few days, Carmen, Finnegan, and even Daisy were more interested in Preston than in Pepper. Preston told stories of all of his adventures at each zoo he had lived at, from San Diego to Singapore.

He told them about the time he surfed outside the San Diego Zoo, the time he went to the top of Pikes Peak outside the Cheyenne Mountain Zoo, and even promised that he had once ridden a dragon in Beijing.

Everyone was excited for a new friend! Pepper, however, was not. He had a strange feeling in his stomach whenever he looked at Preston and his friends laughing and playing.

Suddenly, Pepper had an idea. ***"Maybe if I do a new trick, all my friends will pay attention to me again,"*** he thought.

Pepper flew around the park, collecting every item he needed, then flew over to his friends. He began juggling balls while making silly faces, and his friends smiled and laughed.

Pepper felt great, until, one by one, he began to lose control of the balls, and they all began flying in all directions.

Preston, seeing a chance, swooped under Pepper and with a ***SWOOSH*** caught each one with his magnificent wings. Carmen, Daisy, and Finnegan stared at Preston in awe, enchanted.

Pepper felt his cheeks go red and his eyes sting. He didn't know what this feeling was, and all he wanted to do was run away. As he felt a tear in his eye, Pepper soared quickly to a nearby branch so his friends wouldn't see him cry.

"It's no use," thought Pepper. ***"My gray feathers and I will never stand out, no matter what silly things I do."***

Daisy Dove realized that Pepper was sad, and she tried to make him feel better again. She told him that he didn't need any colorful feathers or tricks or silly hats.

"We love you just the way you are," said Daisy. ***"No more, no less. Just come and play with us!"*** No matter what Daisy did or said, Pepper still felt sad, and that sadness began to fill his heart even more.

Then, from his hideout on that branch, Pepper saw the Big Orange Cat moving slowly towards his gang of friends, ready to attack. No one had noticed yet!

Before Pepper could warn his friends,
the Big Orange Cat jumped into the zoo pen,
hissing at the birds!

As soon as Preston saw the Big Orange Cat, he let out the biggest ***SQUAAAWK*** and began running off back to his box, pushing Carmen, Finnegan, and Daisy in front of the cat to save himself.

Pepper watched it all from his hideout and suddenly, without thinking, flew down as fast as he could to save his friends. ***Swoosh! Swoosh!*** Pepper batted his big wings in Big Orange Cat's face. ***Meowww! Meowww!*** Big Orange Cat growled in annoyance, unable to open his eyes from how fast Pepper was beating his wings.

The Big Orange Cat chased Pepper all around the zoo, nearly catching him a couple of times with his claws. Pepper kept flying and running, making sure the Big Orange Cat was as far away as possible from where his friends were hiding.

Pepper suddenly noticed an empty cage near the other side of the zoo, with enough room between its bars for him, but not for Big Orange Cat! Pepper flew as fast as he could towards it.

As Pepper raced to the cage, Big Orange Cat followed closely behind. Pepper flew gracefully through the bars and with a mighty ***SWOOSH*** of his big wings, he slammed the cage shut. Big Orange Cat was trapped!

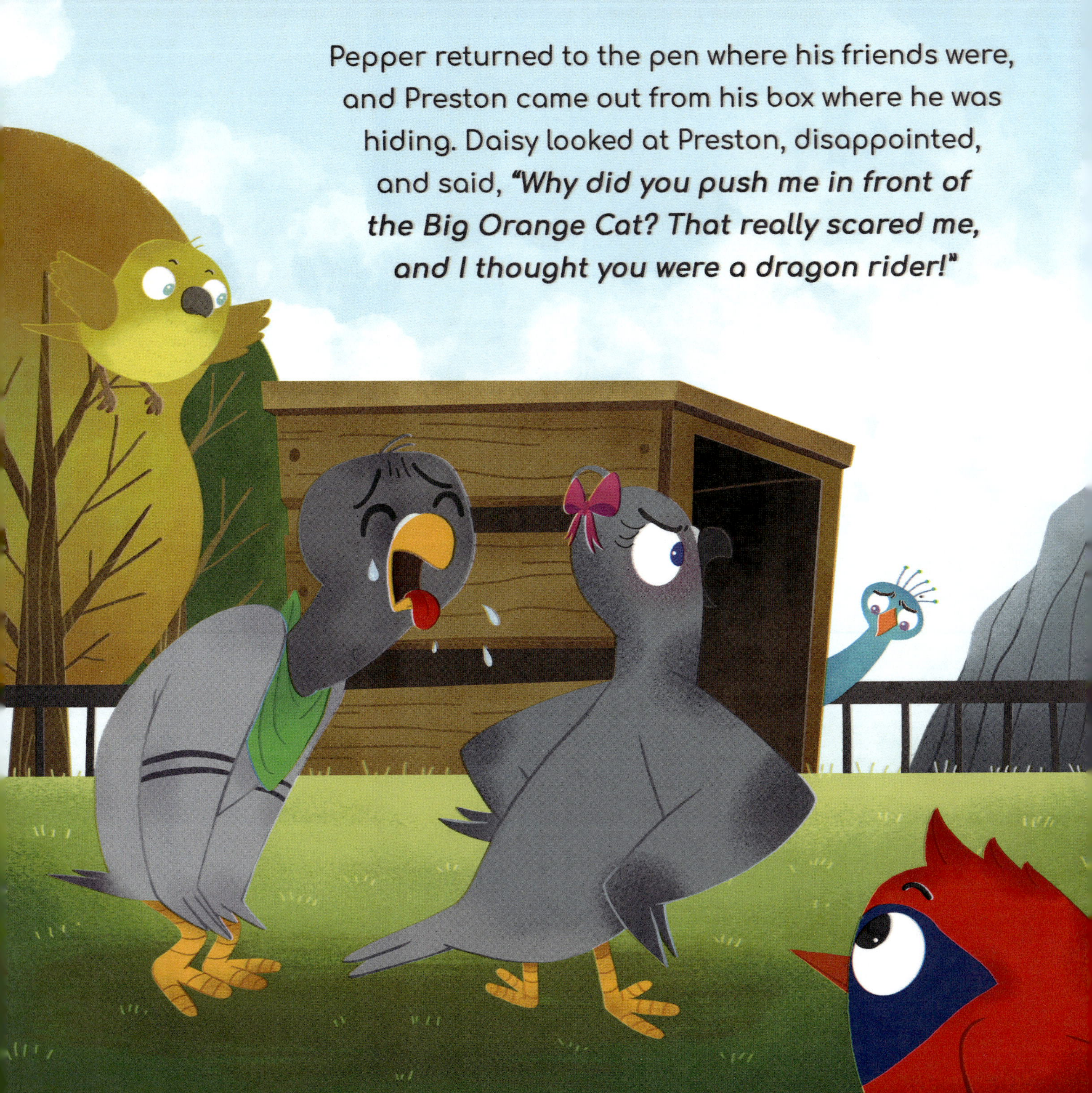

Pepper returned to the pen where his friends were, and Preston came out from his box where he was hiding. Daisy looked at Preston, disappointed, and said, ***"Why did you push me in front of the Big Orange Cat? That really scared me, and I thought you were a dragon rider!"***

Preston looked down and said, ***"I'm sorry. I was nervous about my first day and told a lot of lies. I've only seen a dragon from far away. The Big Orange Cat scared me a lot, but I should have been a better friend and protected you all."***

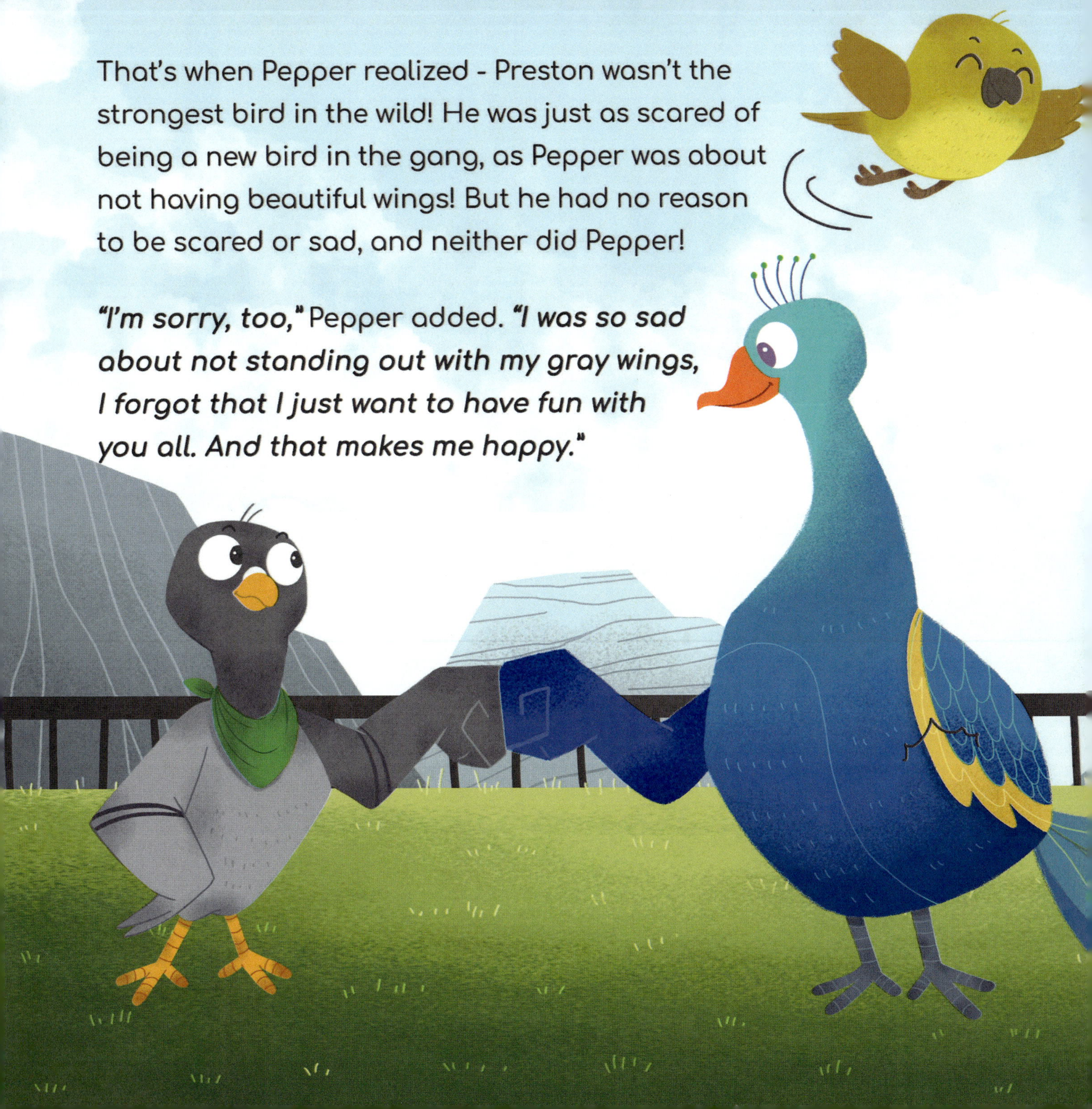

That's when Pepper realized - Preston wasn't the strongest bird in the wild! He was just as scared of being a new bird in the gang, as Pepper was about not having beautiful wings! But he had no reason to be scared or sad, and neither did Pepper!

"I'm sorry, too," Pepper added. *"I was so sad about not standing out with my gray wings, I forgot that I just want to have fun with you all. And that makes me happy."*

"That makes us happy too!" said Carmen and Finnegan.

"Yes, you should love yourself just as you are. We already do!" said Daisy to both Pepper and Preston.

"Pepper, thanks to your big, wonderful feathers," added the thoughtful Daisy Dove, ***"you saved us from the Big Orange Cat!"***

From that day on, Pepper, Preston, Daisy, Carmen, and Finnegan spent their days playing at the zoo together, always thinking of new games to play together. The kindness in their hearts was always more important to them than the brightness of their feathers.

And so, in Birdhattan, lying atop the tallest tree in Central Park, a lesson was learned by our five, feathery friends: The outside doesn't matter, but the inside always does. Never forget to accept yourself and love your friends for who they are!

Made in the USA
Middletown, DE
23 March 2022